# Contents

# Malmö – Facing Europe

Malmö is Sweden's third-largest and most southerly city. It lies so close to Denmark that the Danish capital, Copenhagen, is clearly visible less than ten kilometres away across the Öresund, the stretch of water that separates the two countries. It takes five hours, by train, to reach the Swedish capital, Stockholm, from here and two days to get to the country's northern borders inside the Arctic Circle.

Malmö has always looked to the European mainland for much of its trade. Even before Sweden joined the European Union, on 1 January 1995, the local governments of Malmö in Sweden and Copenhagen in Denmark had begun to co-operate in a regional authority to attract new business and develop the region on both sides of the Öresund.

The 'fixed link' bridge and tunnel between Denmark and Sweden – opened on 1 July 2000 – is a stunning symbol of the success of the Öresund Region. Three million people live here, including over 10,000 scientists working in eleven universities. Its economy is 50 per cent larger than that of the Stockholm region.

Malmö's old, heavy industries have gone. Newer, cleaner service industries are flourishing, and, as part of the unique bi-national Öresund Region, so is Malmö. National and regional governments from around the world are showing a keen interest in this new, but typically Scandinavian, form of international co-operation.

▲ The Öresund Bridge, half of the 'fixed link' between Sweden and Denmark, is 7,845 metres long and has a main span of 490 metres. Pepparholm, a man-made island in the middle of the Öresund, is where the bridge from Sweden becomes a tunnel to Denmark.

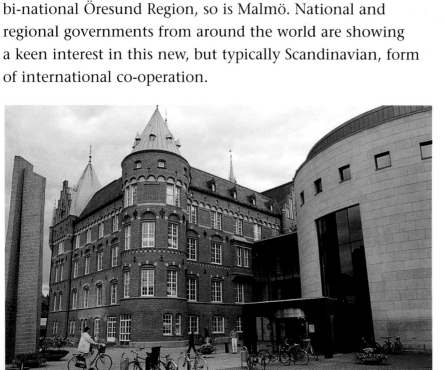

◄ A symbol of Malmö's rebirth, the new city library is an impressive example of how classical and modern Scandinavian architecture can be combined successfully.

◀ This map shows the main geographical features of Sweden, as well as most of the places mentioned in this book.

# SWEDEN: KEY FACTS

**Area:** 449,964 sq km (i.e. slightly larger than California)

**Population:** 8,913,000 (February 2002)

**Population density:** 20 inhabitants per sq km

**Capital city:** Stockholm (750,348)

**Other main cities (municipalities):** Göteborg 466,990; Malmö 259,579; Uppsala 189,569; Linköping 133,168; Västerås 126,328; Örebro 124,207

**Highest mountain:** Kebnekaise (2,111 m)

**Longest river:** Torneälven (510 km)

**Main language:** Swedish

**Major religions:** Evangelical Lutheran (85%)

**Currency:** Krona (Swedish crown, written as SEK; 1 krona = 100 öre)

# 2 Past Times

Swedes are often thought of as a peace-loving people. Sweden has been neutral since the beginning of last century. The country did not fight in either of the two twentieth-century World Wars (1914-18 and 1939-45) and did not join the North Atlantic Treaty Organization (NATO) when it was formed in 1949.

▲ *The Riksdag (Sweden's Parliament), Stockholm.*

However, Sweden's history has not been uneventful. In the Viking period (800-1060) Scandinavian warriors controlled vital trading routes through western Russia and the Baltic States. By the end of the twelfth century Sweden, which included parts of neighbouring Finland, had become a Christian country.

By 1523 Sweden had become a strong, independent country ruled by the powerful King Gustav Vasa (1523-60). Sweden began to develop a successful iron industry producing high quality weapons – swords and cannon – on which it built its military strength. Over the next two centuries Sweden built up a European empire that included the Baltic States and parts of what is today Poland and Germany.

▶ *The* Vasa *(named after Gustav Vasa), built by order of King Gustav II Adolf, and completed in 1628, sank in Stockholm harbour on her maiden voyage. Raised in 1961, the ship has been fully restored to her former glory and can now be seen at the impressive Vasa Museum in Stockholm.*

However, in a series of spectacular military defeats at the beginning of the eighteenth century, Sweden lost most of its foreign territories and, it seems, its appetite for war. There followed almost two centuries of political, industrial and social development at home during which Sweden emerged as one of the richest and most highly-developed countries in the world. The power of the monarchy was gradually dismantled as Swedes built a parliamentary democracy based on equal rights.

▲ *A military band, in ceremonial uniforms dating back to the time of the Swedish empire, marching to the Royal Palace, Stockholm, for the daily changing-of-the-guard ceremony.*

## IN THEIR OWN WORDS

'I'm Stefan Mächler. I work for Malmö's Chamber of Commerce and Industry. Historically, Sweden has been too isolated, for too long. That's why it's been so exciting working here for the last few years. This is a new type of region and it just makes perfect sense to work together with our counterparts in Copenhagen. Now little Malmö can compete with the biggest cities in Europe. The fixed link is not just a symbol of the co-operation between our two countries. It is a reality. It's the thing that makes it so much easier to think of ourselves as one region. It's a fact that we down here are much more international in our thinking than our politicians up in Stockholm. And maybe Stockholm is feeling a bit left out.'

# 3 Landscape and Climate

Sweden is a long, thin and quite sparsely populated country. It extends 1,574 kilometres from north to south. It has 3,218 kilometres of coastline stretching from the Gulf of Bothnia, close to the Arctic Circle, to the North Sea. It shares a 1,619-kilometre land border with Norway to the west, and a 586-kilometre border with Finland to the east.

## Southern and central Sweden

This part of the country is mostly lowland, either flat or with gently sloping hills. Even so, only seven per cent of Sweden's total land surface of 449,964 sq km can be used for agriculture. More than two-thirds (68 per cent) of the country is covered by pine forest (central and northern Sweden) or birch and poplar woodland (far south).

▲ Sweden's forests supply raw materials for the timber and paper industries. The forests are carefully managed. More new trees are planted than are cut down for industrial use.

You are never far from water in Sweden. There are more than 100,000 lakes covering 39,030 sq km. The largest – Lake Vänern, in the south-west – supports a flourishing trout fishing industry.

Sweden is also a land of islands. There are over 25,000 islands in the Stockholm archipelago alone, stretching out across the Baltic Sea, like giant stepping stones, towards Finland.

◀ Sweden is essentially a land of forests and lakes.

## IN THEIR OWN WORDS

'I am Bror Svensson. I am a forest worker from Borlänge. I'm 70 now and I've worked in these forests for 60 years, first with my father, but now practically alone. There were a hundred men here in the 1950s. Today two men do the same work with a couple of machines. I manage forests belonging to several local owners, including the church, and, thank God, they trust me to do a good job – even in the winter, up to my chest in snow. It is all I have ever wanted to do. A man who has never planted a tree has lived without a cause.'

### Northern Sweden

Northern Sweden is mostly covered with forest. Sweden's high mountains (*fjäll*) are all in the far north-west much of which, though beautiful, is cold and inhospitable in winter. Few people live here – the population density in the province of Norrbotten is less than three inhabitants per sq km.

▼ *A snowy taiga landscape, close to Jukkasjärvi in northern Sweden.*

## Midnight sun, midday moon

Because it is so far north, Sweden experiences extreme seasonal contrasts of daylight and darkness. At Abisko, a settlement in the far north of Sweden, the sun never disappears below the horizon between 20 May and 20 July. Even as far south as Stockholm it never gets completely dark at night during June. On the other hand, Sweden has long, dark winters. The people of Abisko never see the sun in December. Even in January it is only above the horizon for about an hour a day.

## A land of all seasons

Although Sweden is located on the same latitude as Canada and stretches far inside the Arctic Circle, it has a surprisingly favourable climate which is influenced by the warm sea currents known as the Gulf Stream. Winter temperatures in Norrbotten often fall well below -30 °C but summer

▼ *The Swedish countryside is at its loveliest in the short summer when Swedes flock to their summer cottages, most of which are close to a river, a lake or the coast.*

temperatures can rise above +30 °C. The average summer temperature of 15 °C for Umeå, in the north, is only two degrees lower than Malmö's average summer temperature. Even in winter, Umeå (-6 °C) is, on average, only eight degrees colder than Malmö (+2 °C), a thousand kilometres to the south.

The winters are long and cold and the summers short and wet. July, August and September are the wettest months with an average rainfall of around 75 mm each month. February and March are the driest months with a monthly average of around 35 mm, which, at that time of year, usually falls as snow.

▲ *Swedes make the most of the snow during their long winters. Cross-country skiing is a national sport and the snowmobile is not only an excellent form of off-road transport, it is also used for racing.*

## IN THEIR OWN WORDS

'I'm Fredrik Annell, aged 34, and I am an art director in a Stockholm advertising agency. Like most Swedes, I like to make the most of our short summers. I work longer hours during the winter months so that I can take the summer off. It helps that I can work online from my summer cottage if I have to. I can't believe there was ever a time without computers. How did we do anything, back then? I'm responsible for IT at one of Sweden's top three agencies. We have some of the highest profile multi-nationals as customers. But we must take care. You have to concentrate on what you're best at. In this business you can be a millionaire tonight and a pauper tomorrow morning.'

# Natural Resources

## Mining

Sweden's early wealth was built on its massive reserves of iron ore and copper. Today, however, the huge coppermines at Falun, in Dalarna, are long ago worked-out and have instead become an important tourist attraction as a major industrial museum.

## Energy

Oil, hydroelectricity and nuclear power are Sweden's principal sources of energy. However, Sweden is not rich in natural energy resources and so has to import more than three-quarters of all its energy raw materials.

In a country which is technologically advanced – half the population own a mobile phone and almost two-thirds use the Internet – energy consumption is naturally high. Sweden is also cold – around a quarter of all Sweden's annual energy consumption is used to heat homes, workplaces and other buildings.

## Oil

Sweden has no oil of its own. Oil consumption, however, accounts for over one third of the country's total energy supply. Every litre of petrol or diesel used in every vehicle in Sweden has to be imported.

▼ *An oil refinery and storage depot, Stockholm.*

## Hydroelectricity

The great rivers of northern Sweden generate 64 terawatts (TW) of electricity in a normal year, depending on rainfall. The most productive river is the Luleälv which has 15 hydropower stations.

## Nuclear power

Sweden has 11 nuclear reactors in four nuclear power stations. However, Swedes are concerned about the safety of nuclear reactors and nuclear waste, which has to be stored in specially sealed vaults. Following the meltdown at the Chernobyl reactor in the Ukraine in 1986, which devastated Sweden's reindeer farming industry and affected food production and tourism in the north, Sweden's energy policy for the twenty-first century is to work towards phasing out all its nuclear power stations.

▶ *Wind-generated electrical power is produced by these giant windmills that are situated around Sweden's windiest coasts, in the south.*

# IN THEIR OWN WORDS

'I'm Robert Jacobsson, I'm 46 and I'm a builder from Uppsala. Our climate is harsh so we need to build well. Wood is a good material for us because our climate is rather dry. By law all new buildings in Sweden have to be well-insulated, triple glazed and energy-efficient. In our firm we specialize in under-floor heating. We lay plastic pipes onto the concrete, then put the wooden floor on top. The pipes carry warm water. It's much cheaper than burning a lot of oil to heat large radiators. The heat from the floor rises to heat the whole room. Even in winter you can walk on our floors without shoes and socks on.'

## Agriculture

Half of Sweden is covered by forest. About one third of the rest is hills and mountains, lakes and marshland. Less than one tenth of Sweden's total land area can be used by farmers. The climate severely limits what can be grown. About 40 per cent of farmland is used to grow barley, wheat and oats. Potatoes are grown throughout the country and sugar beet is grown in the south. Vodka, which can be made from cereals or potatoes, is Sweden's biggest processed food export.

Most Swedish farms are still family-owned and worked by family members. But the number of people employed in agriculture is falling steadily. Fewer than 3 per cent of the working population of Sweden are employed on farms.

▲ *Oilseed rape is a relatively new crop to be grown on Swedish farms.*

## New markets

Almost three-quarters of Sweden's agricultural products go to the food processing industry. When Sweden joined the EU in 1995, it gained access to new markets in Europe. Today it is quite usual to find Swedish chocolates, baked goods, frozen vegetables and margarine in our supermarkets.

◀ *Sweden produces 3.3 million tonnes of milk annually. Milk is an important part of the Swedish diet and is commonly drunk daily at mealtimes by adults as well as children.*

# IN THEIR OWN WORDS

'I am Julie Skogs, a 40-year-old farmer from Leksand. There's no status in being a farmer today. You're nothing if you don't work with computers. This farm's been in my husband's family for over 250 years and with seventy-four cows we're a big farm for this area. These used to be farming communities. Now there are maybe one or two farms per village. Everyone's gone to the cities. And that means we have a labour problem. It's a very short growing season up here. The weather isn't kind to us, either. So we have to get the hay cut and dried very quickly. Which means we need extra help, but only at certain times. No one wants to do farm work. Our sons aren't interested, so we have no idea who'll inherit this place.'

## Forestry

Sweden is, above all else, a land of pine forests. It exports one tenth of all the world's forest products, is the fourth largest exporter of paper, the third largest exporter of pulp, and the second largest exporter of pine wood products, in the world. A third of all European newspapers and magazines are printed on Swedish paper.

The forests are, however, much more than just a source of raw material for industry. They are a natural resource in the widest sense and are carefully protected by Swedish law so that everyone can enjoy them.

▼ *Logs being transported from the forest, where they have just been cut down and stripped, to a nearby paper mill.*

# 5

# The Changing Environment

## A natural affinity

Swedes feel close to their natural environment. The national anthem praises Sweden's mountains, meadows, sky and sun rather than the king or famous military victories from the past. Sweden was the first country in Europe to introduce state-owned national parks – an idea taken taken from the great national parks of the United States. Their aim is to protect areas of outstanding natural value or beauty from exploitation and development. Today there are 26 of them, including Ekoparken, the world's first national city park, in Stockholm.

## Retreat from the countryside

At the beginning of the twentieth century fewer than one-third of Swedes lived in towns or cities. Today, fewer than 18 per cent live in the countryside. Farming has declined dramatically while industry has expanded. Rural villages, especially in the remote areas north of Stockholm, have slowly emptied while urban areas have grown rapidly.

▲ This beautiful area is very close to Sweden's capital city, Stockholm.

## IN THEIR OWN WORDS

'I am Günther Löfgren, I'm 63 and I'm a Stockholm hotel proprietor. Our hotel is less than a five-minute walk from the city centre but you could be deep in the countryside, it's so quiet. We have relatively low noise pollution in Sweden. That surprises a lot of our foreign visitors. They don't expect it to be so clean and tidy, either. Or so warm in the summer. They expect to see polar bears in the street! We like quiet, I think. We are perhaps a little too reserved, though. There are many Swedes, especially from the north and west, who are extremely conservative and don't much like Sweden being in the EU, and absolutely don't want the Euro. Personally, I think we should publicize our country more and encourage tourism. We are an enormous country. We're not going to destroy the environment by building a few more hotels, are we?'

Northern Sweden is now officially recognized by the European Union as a Sparsely Populated Region.

Such rapid growth of towns and cities puts enormous pressure on the environment. The population of Göteborg (Gothenburg) more than doubled between 1920 and 2000. Industrial cities of the Swedish 'midlands', such as Örebro and Västerås, grew fourfold in size over the same period, swallowing up land that was needed for new factories, homes, schools, hospitals and roads.

▼ *Sergels Torg, a central plaza in downtown Stockholm. To the right is Kulturhuset, Stockholm's arts centre, which incorporates theatres, cinemas, exhibition spaces, a public library, shops, cafés and meeting places.*

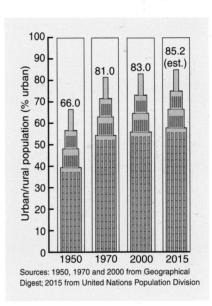

Sources: 1950, 1970 and 2000 from Geographical Digest; 2015 from United Nations Population Division

▲ *Sweden is a very urban society, a trend which is set to continue.*

## Problems and solutions

In 1930 there were 60 inhabitants per private car in Sweden. By 2002 that figure had fallen to 1.3 people per car. Sweden has strict traffic pollution laws – it is illegal, for example, to sit in a parked car with the engine running – and has developed one of the world's most efficient public transport systems. Its small population and huge land area make environmental controls easy to impose inside the country but they cannot prevent international pollution drifting across from other heavily industrialized European countries, such as Britain, Germany, Poland and the Baltic States.

▶ *All Swedish cities and most of the bigger towns have excellent networks of well-built cycle routes. Unfortunately, not all cyclists wear helmets.*

# IN THEIR OWN WORDS

'My name's Johann Amri. I'm a 22-year-old student from Sundsvall. I hate graffiti on walls and on the *tunnelbana* (underground railway). It just looks a mess. Stockholm is beautiful. People should have the right to a pleasant local environment as well as a clean national and international one. I've got this job as a graffiti hunter while I'm a student. It's well paid and it's not dangerous. You just have to watch out for suspicious-looking characters. If they take out a spray can you approach them and ask them to stop. Usually, they do. If they don't, you can get a bit heavy but you're not supposed to assault anyone, of course. I have a mobile and can get extra help in just a couple of minutes if I need it. Usually, I don't. I'm fully trained in several martial arts.'

Many Swedish forests and lakes have been damaged by acid rain caused by pollution. The source of more than half of the measured industrial pollution in Sweden lies outside the country's borders. The Swedish government campaigns energetically for worldwide reductions in air, land and marine pollution.

▲ *Spraying agricultural lime into a lake to counteract the damage caused by acid rain. Lime neutralizes the acidity of the water.*

## Power from water

Hydroelectric power stations are an efficient source of electrical energy. However, building hydroelectric dams changes the natural balance. Lake Vänern used to be a very productive salmon-spawning ground in Sweden until hydroelectric dams were built in the 1950s and 1960s. The salmon were almost extinct by 1975.

In 1998 the Swedish Parliament voted to prevent any further development along the four remaining great 'wild and scenic' rivers of the far north – the Vindelälven, Piteälven, Kalixälven and Torneälven – which together might have been harnessed to produce large amounts of electricity.

### A unique freedom

Swedish law allows everyone in Sweden (not just Swedish citizens) a unique degree of access to the countryside. This ancient law is called *Allemansrätten*, or the Right of Common Access. Anyone can use national parks and public footpaths, but they can also use privately owned forests and other land, rivers and lakes. You may walk, hike, cycle, ski or ride, take a rest, have a picnic, camp overnight, swim, canoe or sail – all without the need for permission or the fear of trespassing.

There are, of course, some conditions. You must respect the interests and privacy of landowners and tenants. You must not damage the environment: forest fires are easily started. Many species of wild flowers are protected by law from being picked. And you must not disturb natural habitats or endanger animals: some, such as bears and wolves, are very rare and also potentially dangerous to humans.

Swedish pupils are taught about environmental protection from the first year of school. It is unusual, therefore, to find much litter, either in towns or in the countryside in Sweden.

▲ *Everyone has the right of access to all of Sweden's countryside. It is important, however, to act responsibly and to behave with consideration for the environment and the landowner's interests.*

◄ *Recycling centres for paper and cartons, different types of glass, batteries and cans are located in every Swedish community. Sweden was one of the first countries in the world to introduce communal recycling collection points. Household rubbish has to be sorted into different types too, and is collected separately.*

Swedes enjoy mushroom- and berry-picking in the autumn and are free to take what they need. As more tourists visit Sweden, occasional newspaper stories report disagreements between local people and 'foreigners' who are sometimes accused of hunting, mushroom-picking and berry-picking in industrial quantities.

▶ *Sweden's wild flower meadows offer an abundance of species, many of which are under threat elsewhere in Europe. Rare, protected varieties may not be picked.*

## IN THEIR OWN WORDS

'Hi. I'm Linda Hjorth (right), 20, from Västerås and this is my friend Elinor Iderall. We're both students. A lot of us sell papers on the street to earn a bit extra, but only in the summer. It's far too cold in winter. I guess you could say that this newspaper I'm selling today is part of the junk problem we'll have to deal with tomorrow. But here in Sweden we all have different boxes at home for different types of rubbish. It's all collected and most of it is recycled. In fact, in the last 15 years or so it's become very sophisticated with different kinds of plastics and different types of glass all collected separately. And paper and card and cans and batteries! People here are very aware of this problem. We know we can't just go on using up all the world's resources and piling up our junk everywhere.'

# 6

# The Changing Population

## Who are the Swedes?

When we think of Swedes, we may have a mental picture of people who are tall, blonde and blue-eyed. And perhaps also reserved, unemotional and serious-minded. Indigenous Swedes, like most Scandinavians, do tend to be taller and fairer than, for example, southern Europeans. However, the Sami (or Lapps) who have inhabited northern Europe since ancient times and who form an important cultural and linguistic minority in northern Sweden have very different physical features.

Today there are between 18,000 and 20,000 Sami in Sweden. Most have given up their traditional, nomadic reindeer-herding way of life in the last 30 years and moved to cities where they can earn more and enjoy a higher standard of living. The Sami way of life is threatened more by economic than by social change in Sweden.

## What Swedes value

Swedish society is strongly influenced by Swedes' love of order and fairness. The Swedish word *lagom* represents a fundamental concept not expressed in many other cultures. It means 'just about right', neither too much nor too little, comfortable. Most Swedes strive to achieve *lagom* in their lives. Behaviour such as losing your temper in public, displaying your wealth by buying an ostentatious car, and disobeying rules is not thought acceptable in Sweden. However, dramatic changes in Sweden's population over the last half century are having a profound impact on what it means to be Swedish today.

▲ *Not all Swedes are tall, blonde and blue-eyed, but these girls represent many people's idea of a typical Swede.*

▼ Midsommar *(Midsummer)* is the most important celebration of the Swedish year, and is celebrated in every community in the country. After the majstång *(Maypole)* has been decorated with birch twigs, it is erected in the centre of the village. This is followed by the playing of traditional music, with singing and dancing, which often continues through the longest day until the early hours.

▲ In the central Swedish province of Dalarna every village has its own traditional costume. These costumes were once in daily use. Today, they are only worn for special occasions, such as weddings and at Midsommar *celebrations.*

## IN THEIR OWN WORDS

'My name is Kerstin Reuterborg. I am 38 and come from Nusnäs. I am a Dalarna horse painter. In the old days, in the remote forests of Dalarna, working ponies used to drag felled timber to the riverbank or lakeside where it was floated down to a mill. The foresters used to carve pieces of wood into the shape of these ponies. Only a horse made and painted here in Nusnäs is a true Dalarna horse. It's a symbol of this part of Sweden and we're very proud of it. In a typical day I paint about 150. I've been doing this for fifteen years. I guess I've painted half a million Dalarna horses. Boring? Absolutely not. I think of each one as an individual.'

## Emigrants...

Between 1850 and 1930 one-and-a-half million Swedes – about one in six of the population – emigrated to North America to escape economic depression and social unrest at home. Even today almost every indigenous Swedish family has at least one distant North American relative.

## ...and immigrants

However, from the 1930s, as employment opportunities, social conditions, healthcare and housing improved greatly in Sweden, immigrants began to outnumber emigrants. At first, most 'immigrants' were returnees, victims of the Great Depression of the 1930s in the United States. But by 1957 foreign immigrants accounted for 5 per cent of the population. In Europe, only Switzerland has a higher proportion of immigrants.

## Sweden and racism

From the 1950s most immigrants were eastern European and Finnish 'guest workers'. By the 1970s, though, Swedish industry no longer needed guest workers, and immigration was mainly limited to asylum seekers and other refugees, principally from South America and the Middle East. During the 1980s and 1990s the number of

▲ *It is not unusual for white Swedish couples to adopt non-white children.*

▼ *Many of Sweden's immigrants, like these market traders, make a living from their own businesses.*

# IN THEIR OWN WORDS

'I'm Oula Keskitalo, a Sami reindeer farmer from Kiruna. I think we are Sweden's forgotten people, Europe's forgotten people maybe. Although Europe seems a long way from here. My parents lived and travelled with their herds. Stockholm was a foreign city to them. Today we don't follow the herds. We just take a short helicopter flight every now and then to check they're OK. There's no money in this. No future. My kids'd be crazy to stay in this business. My daughter's a journalist – wants to be a proper writer, wants to write about Sami culture so it's not completely lost. My son's a truck driver – drives to Spain every week. Comes back with good wine and a suntan. Imagine, he's a Sami who hates the snow!'

asylum seekers grew rapidly. Today every twentieth person in Sweden is a foreign citizen, every tenth was born outside the country.

The combination of large numbers of immigrants, the decline of the Swedish economy in the 1990s and a steep rise in unemployment has made some indigenous Swedes question their liberal traditions of tolerance. Some people feel that their cultural identity as Swedes is threatened and there have been incidents of racial persecution, and calls for a complete halt to immigration into the country.

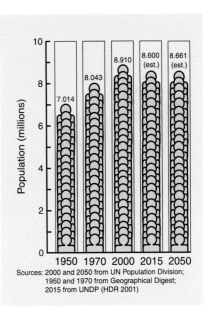

It is predicted that the population of Sweden will decline slightly over the next few decades.

Sources: 2000 and 2050 from UN Population Division; 1950 and 1970 from Geographical Digest; 2015 from UNDP (HDR 2001)

◀ *Sweden today is a multi-racial country. One in eight children in Sweden is born to parents of foreign origin.*

▲ *It is predicted that the population of Sweden will decline slightly over the next few decades.*

## An ageing population

Sweden enjoys a high standard of living. Unemployment is relatively low. Families are small. Less than one fifth of the population is under 15. By contrast, with its excellent provision of care for the elderly Sweden has one of the oldest populations in the world. It is estimated that there will be 2.1 million Swedes over 65 by 2025.

## A language under threat?

In March 2002 the Swedish Government issued a formal, legal declaration that Swedish was the official language of Sweden. In Sweden most multi-national companies have adopted English as the company language. Many now even do business inside Sweden in English! It is compulsory to learn English in Swedish schools and it has been estimated that more people in Sweden speak English, per head of population, than in Britain.

Language is fundamental to identity. All immigrants to Sweden have the right to free Swedish lessons during their normal working hours. Moreover, the children at school also have the right to study or continue studying their mother tongue.

## Diversity or difference?

Sweden is in a state of flux. The population is mixed – less 'Swedish' than it was even twenty years ago. Many immigrants are still isolated by their culture and their lack of Swedish. Most people live in cities in the south. Many northern country-dwellers feel remote and forgotten.

▲ *The provision of care for the elderly in Sweden ranks alongside the best in the world.*

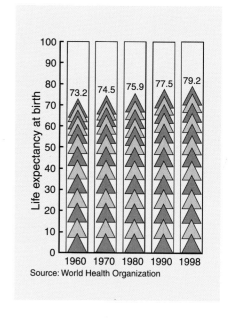

Source: World Health Organization

▲ *Life expectancy for Swedes is high and rising.*

Some of the elderly find it difficult to understand or accept new behaviours and living patterns, while some young people think that Sweden offers fewer opportunities than her European neighbours.

◄ *Sweden is rapidly becoming a multi-cultural society. However, some small right-wing political parties have appeared in recent years which campaign against the country's liberal immigration policies.*

## IN THEIR OWN WORDS

'My name is Louisa Friberg and I'm a 23-year-old traditional fiddle player from Steninge. I do this because I love the music. I'm Swedish and this music is deep inside me. Swedish folk music's a bit like the Scottish and Irish stuff – a bit sadder-sounding, maybe. I sing in Swedish because these songs are traditional, with no translations. You can't translate old folk songs! I play in a little band called *Norr om Stan* (North of the City) 'cos that's where we're all from, north of Stockholm. I play at weddings, and, of course, there's always lots of work at *Midsommar*. It's cool with this music, you know in regional costume, and everyone's happy 'cos it's *Midsommar*, and that's when Sweden is most Swedish.'

# 7 Changes at Home

**Family life, as is was...**

In no other European country has home life and the structure of the family changed so rapidly as in Sweden. As recently as the 1930s very large families in small rural communities were the norm. Men worked on the land. They were the sole breadwinners. Women married, had children, looked after the home, and were not expected to go out to work.

The state Lutheran (Protestant) church, into which all Swedes were born, was a powerful influence on people's lives. You were expected to be modest and God-fearing, to work hard and go to church, to marry and have children. Divorce was practically unheard of. Having children outside marriage was a scandal and brought disgrace to the woman and shame to her family.

◄ *The main religion is Lutheran Protestant, but in Sweden today there are a growing number of mosques, temples and other places of religious worship.*

# IN THEIR OWN WORDS

'Hi. I'm Håkan Jonsson, a 13-year-old school pupil from Uppsala. There are twenty-two of us in my class. Three, including me, have parents who are married for the first time and are still together. Everyone else has parents who are separated, divorced, remarried or unmarried. But it's really no big deal here. Even my grandma agrees now. My mum's from Australia and when she first met my dad my grandma was really shocked that he could think about marrying a foreigner. Then she met her and realized that she was no different from a Swede – except she couldn't speak Swedish, of course. The big advantage is that I grew up speaking English as well as Swedish. I always get top marks in every English test.'

## ...and is now

Today, half of all children in Sweden are born outside marriage. Around 20 per cent of couples with children choose to remain unmarried, and almost half of all marriages end in divorce. Nonetheless, 78 per cent of children under 18 live with both their biological parents, 14 per cent live with one parent, and 7 per cent live in so-called 'mixed' families where one parent is living with a new partner. This means that around 20 per cent of under 18s have parents who are separated or divorced, and around 8 per cent of under 18s have never lived with both biological parents.

▶ *Fewer Swedes are choosing to get married and half of all children are born to unmarried parents.*

## At home in Sweden

Their homes are very important to Swedes. They are usually well-built, spacious and comfortable. Home is still where Swedes spend the important annual celebrations of *Midsommar* and Christmas. Although eating out is becoming more popular, especially among the young, many Swedes still prefer to entertain at home.

▲ *Strandvägen, one of central Stockholm's most fashionable boulevards, is lined with yachts and houseboats.*

There are just over four million households in Sweden. The average size of a household is 2.1 persons. However, a substantial proportion of the population (40 per cent) live alone – a figure which has been rising steadily since the 1980s.

A little under half of all Swedes live in apartments, usually purpose-built to very high standards. All Sweden's older apartments, mostly in centrally-located areas of the larger towns and cities, have been renovated in the last 30 years. People who live in apartments in Sweden can expect to enjoy communal gardens and play areas, space for car parking and bicycle storage, laundry facilities and even a sauna.

◄ *1920s' apartment blocks in Stockholm.*

## IN THEIR OWN WORDS

'I'm a 20-year-old student from Södertälje called Mikaela Ledin. In my family we hardly ever see each other during the week. Dad works, mum works, I'm at college and my brother's at school. In the evenings Dad brings work home, mum works part-time in a restaurant, I sometimes stay at college to work in the library, and my brother's always at an ice hockey match, or out some place with his girlfriend. Even at the weekends we rarely see each other. Maybe that's one reason why family celebrations at Christmas and Lucia and especially at *Midsommar* are so important to us. I don't think I'm much of a family person but I could never spend *Midsommar* abroad or even away from my family. It just wouldn't be right. You just couldn't do it. It's not Swedish!'

About 40 per cent of the population live in rented accommodation, 20 per cent own their houses or apartments and the rest live in tenant-owners' flats.

There are 400,000 summer cottages in Sweden, mostly in quiet country areas or on coastal islands. Most families have access to a summer cottage. It is part of what it means to be Swedish to be able to travel to these havens and spend the short, light summer away from the noise and the bustle of city life.

▼ *A typical summer cottage offers a welcome retreat far away from city life.*

## Looking after the children

Modern Sweden, where it has been illegal to hit, threaten or in any other way persecute children since 1979, is a very good country to grow up in.

One in five of the population is under 18, and since 1993 they have had a children's ombudsman (*Barnombudsmannen*) whose job it is to safeguard their rights and interests as set out in the *UN Convention on the Rights of the Child*. The ombudsman communicates directly with young people by questionnaire, letter and telephone, and on a dedicated Internet website called Children's Channel where young Swedes can find out about their rights.

▲ *All parents have the right to professional day-care for their children while they are out at work.*

## Off to school

Schools are provided and organized by local authorities but financed and controlled by the state during the nine years of compulsory schooling from 7-16. Almost all pupils (98 per cent) go on to the three-year upper-secondary school and most join after-school clubs or classes for sports, music or

◄ *One in three 9-14-year-olds in Sweden is learning to play a musical instrument.*

other non-academic activities. Only 3 per cent of pupils attend independent schools in Sweden.

English is compulsory in Swedish schools, and over one-third of school children start studying it in first grade. Swedes today (and not only young Swedes) are among the best non-native speakers of English in the world. Pupils who speak a language other than Swedish at home are entitled to seven years of tuition in that language at school. School meals are free to all pupils during the first nine years at school.

▶ *Swedes make the most of the summer months to meet outdoors. Winters are usually too severe for an enjoyable street life.*

# IN THEIR OWN WORDS

'My name's Birgitta Dalin. I'm 53 and I work as a secondary school teacher in Leksand, Dalarna. I had lots of brothers and sisters, and we all had the same parents and the same surname and we were local people, like everyone else in the village. Today it's not like that any more. My students come from Vietnam and Jordan and Iran and Turkey, and Sweden, too, of course. Many have one Swedish parent. But some have parents who are not Swedish at all. Sure, it causes a few problems with language and cultural differences. But actually it makes life up here a lot more cosmopolitan and interesting than it would otherwise be. Many of our students are from what used to be called 'broken homes'. But no one talks like that – or even thinks like that, I hope – any more.'

### Fair treatment for all

Less than a century ago Sweden was one of the poorest countries in Europe. However, during the twentieth century only the Japanese economy grew faster. Today, Sweden is one of the richest countries in the world.

Only twice – in 1976 and 1991 – have Swedes not re-elected Social Democratic Party governments since 1932. Social Democratic policies have been based on two fundamental principles – co-operation and equality. Instead of nationalizing important industries and services, as in other Socialist countries, Swedish governments have preferred to co-operate with private companies to help them increase their profitability. At the same time successive governments have used progressive laws to make sure that the country's wealth is distributed fairly and evenly among the population.

### A nation of high tax payers

In modern Sweden, there is no real poverty. Sweden is a welfare state. The government takes money from its citizens in the form of income tax, VAT and other taxes and uses it to provide free child care, education, health care and social benefits for all. Swedes pay high taxes. Those who earn more pay more. This is an important way of creating a more equal society. Paying over 50 per cent of your total earnings in tax is not unusual in Sweden. In return Swedes benefit from reliable and environmentally friendly public transport, good roads, efficient public

▲ *Drivers must use their lights – even during the hours of daylight. This is an example of Sweden's progressive approach to road safety. Sweden was the first country to make the wearing of seat belts compulsory, too.*

◀ *This Volvo ambulance can deliver state-of-the-art paramedic treatment and a fast, comfortable ride to hospital. Hospitals are modern, efficient and offer world-class healthcare to all citizens.*

◄ *This Malmö bus is powered by natural gas which produces less pollution than petrol- or diesel-powered vehicles.*

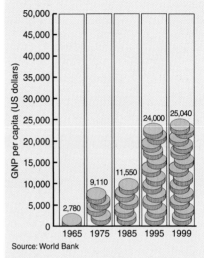

Source: World Bank

services and generous social benefits. Every town has a public sports hall with an outdoor ice hockey pitch and indoor tennis courts. Their hospitals are among the best in the world. Their schools provide an excellent broad education. Road safety is exceptionally high. The crime rate is relatively low.

▲ *National wealth per head of population is slowly rising now after a big jump at the start of the 1990s.*

## IN THEIR OWN WORDS

'I'm Frederik Västberg, an 18-year-old ice hockey player from Leksand. This is not a good time for ice hockey here. It's the first time since the 1950s we've been out of the premier league. A decade ago Sweden won gold at the Olympics and all the best players were from Leksand. Today we're in the second division. But it's still the only sport worth playing in Leksand. You have to train hard – in the gym and on the ice – every day of the year. You've got to be fearless and strong and, of course, a good skater. If you're good, you can earn SEK 100,000 a month at the top. I've got a smart car and a nice flat. And maybe ten more years playing. Then I guess I'll coach.'

## Looking after the very young...

Since the 1970s more and more women have joined the workforce. Today the vast majority of Swedish mothers (and fathers) have a full-time job. So the government has made childcare a priority. Since 1995 all local authorities have had to provide high quality, professional and inexpensive childcare for every child between 18 months and school age who needs it.

## ...the sick...

All who live in Sweden are covered by its national health service. If you become ill, or even have to stay home to look after a sick child, you will receive a daily allowance of up to 80 per cent of your lost earnings. Swedes pay for medicine and even to visit the doctor, but only up to a maximum of around SEK 1,000 (£72) for medical treatment and SEK 1,500 (£110) for drugs, per year. After that, all treatment and drugs are free.

▲ *Swedish schoolteachers (left) dress casually and pupils address them by their first names.*

◄ *Most elderly people in Sweden live alone. It is unusual to find grandparents, for example, living with their family. However, elderly people living alone who become ill are well looked after in daycare centres or residential hospitals as part of Sweden's welfare state provision.*

# IN THEIR OWN WORDS

'I am Ingeborg Krensler. I am 93 years old and come from Alvesta. I retired as a teacher of art and am now a pensioner. I moved to this care home when my husband died. We all have everything we need. It's wonderful, really. I have my own room, with a bathroom, and my own TV. I can be very independent but I have all the help I need if I want it. Part of my pension pays for this. But we've all paid already, haven't we? With our high taxes. The highest in the world. My husband and I both worked all our lives. We used to travel abroad a lot but we were always glad to get back to Sweden where everything's clean and tidy, and everything works properly.'

## ...and the very old

A hundred years ago most elderly Swedes lived in poor, overcrowded accommodation. Today elderly Swedes have one of the highest standards of living among pensioners anywhere in the world. One in five Swedes is an old age pensioner, and all of them are entitled to an old age pension – most from the age of 65 – under Sweden's complicated pension rules. There are generous housing, health and incapacity benefits, a home help service and good homes for those who can no longer look after themselves.

◄ *All Swedes receive a state pension which allows the elderly to live in comfort and security.*

# 8

# Changes at Work

## From the farm to the factory

Sweden was a poor agricultural economy until well into the twentieth century, but there was some early industrialization. The world's oldest limited company, Stora, was founded at the copper mine in Falun over 700 years ago. Small-scale ironworking communities grew up around ore deposits or near large lakes or rivers. Towns or villages based around a single company were common and can still be found in Sweden today. The company – a mine, foundry or factory – provided work, simple homes, perhaps a school, a clinic and a general store, and offered a kind of life-long security within a small and often remote community.

▲ *Swedish farming is modern and efficient. Animals are well-cared-for in clean and comfortable conditions.*

In the nineteenth century, Sweden began to develop modern industries. Gustav Pasch invented the safety match in Sweden. Lars Magnus Ericsson developed telephone technology, and Alfred Nobel invented dynamite. Large numbers of people moved from farms to jobs in the new factories and a new class of urban industrial worker was formed.

◄ *Sweden is very much a trading nation. Most of its exports are transported by sea.*

The Social Democratic Party, which formed successive Swedish governments, encouraged and supported industrial workers in trade unions from the 1930s. The resulting stability in labour relations helped Swedish industry and business to prosper during the twentienth century.

The new Malmö-Copenhagen Region (see pages 4-5) is not the first example of Swedish-Danish co-operation. Back in 1874, the first Swedish trade union was established, for tobacco packers in Malmö, by Danish workers who were concerned to keep wage levels high.

▶ *Sweden's rail network is electrified. Trains are modern and clean but rail travel in Sweden is the second most expensive in Europe, after Britain.*

## IN THEIR OWN WORDS

'I'm Glenn Mollergren, aged 29, and I come from Göteborg. I'm a labour relations journalist. My grandfather was a tinker from Romania, among the first modern immigrants to Sweden, in fact. As a boy my dad wasn't allowed to play with the neighbours' kids because he was a "gypsy". Perhaps that's why I became a union man. I can't walk away from injustice. Sweden has had quite good labour relations for a long time but I think there's been a shift of power away from workers to management. Some of the bigger unions in Sweden today seem more interested in political influence than in improving the working conditions of ordinary people in factories and offices. One reason I became a journalist was so that I could expose that sort of thing.'

## All play and no work?

Around five million people in Sweden are employed. Women make up more than half the population and just under half the workforce, and they have the legal right to work in all occupations, including the armed forces.

Women also have the right to equal pay in Sweden. However, because more women work part-time and fewer reach the very highest-paid jobs, women still earn slightly less than men in Sweden. But the gap is closing.

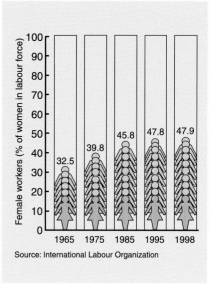

Source: International Labour Organization

▲ *Female workers make up almost half of the total workforce.*

◀ *Swedish women enjoy more equality of opportunity than in any other country in the world.*

Every employed person in Sweden is entitled to a minimum of five weeks paid holiday per year. Some get more. Stockholm practically empties during July as families flock to their summer cottages to enjoy the all-too-short summer. There are thirteen additional official public holidays, including *Midsommar*, and, increasingly, the day before each one is taken as a half-day off.

▶ *More mobile phones are owned per head of population in Sweden than anywhere else around the globe.*

# IN THEIR OWN WORDS

'My name is Charlie Annell. I'm 63 and a retired newspaper editor from Malmö. Not so long ago you worked, here in Sweden, for one company all your working life. It was normal: thirty years or more. And it was even common for companies to ask you to stay on one more year after retirement age. Now everyone wants to take early retirement, to have a chance to live a little, to travel maybe, anyway to do something else after the working life is finished and while you're still healthy. We're all living longer, too. And that's putting very great stress on the social welfare system that Sweden is famous for. If I live to, say, 90, that's twenty-five years the Swedish state will have been paying out a pension to me – after I have stopped earning and contributing.'

Parents can take 450 days (15 months) maternity or paternity leave on up to 80 per cent of their full salary. Fathers can take an additional ten days off work, with full pay, when a child is born. All parents with children under eight are entitled to reduce their working day by two hours (with corresponding loss of pay, of course) if they choose.

So when does the work get done? Swedes are generally hard-working and often put in long hours at work – especially during their dark winters. It is not unusual to start work at 6.30 or 7.00 am.

▼ *Stockholm's oldest coffee shop, in Stockholm's Old Town. Swedes do know how to relax, especially when the sun shines.*

## From ships to microchips

By the middle of the twentieth century Swedish industry was amongst the most successful in the world. For such a small country, Sweden was home to a staggering number of big industrial names. Names such as AGA (gas), Alfa-Laval (farm machinery), ASEA (engineering), Astra (medicines), Electrolux (vacuum cleaners and white goods), Ericsson (telecommunications equipment), Hasselblad (cameras), Saab (aircraft, cars and trucks), SKF (steel ball-bearings) and Volvo (cars, trucks, buses and marine engines).

During Sweden's economic crisis of the 1990s most of these companies were bought out by foreign businesses. The new multi-national owners of these companies are less involved in Sweden and its economy and politics than the original founders were. They run their businesses for maximum profit and cut their workforces when they need to. Unemployment was an unpleasant new experience for many Swedes at the turn of the millennium. The government lost tax income and, at the same time, had to pay out increased amounts in unemployment benefit.

▼ *A relic of the past? A lightship under refit in an otherwise deserted dry-dock in Malmö, which used to be a thriving ship-building city.*

# IN THEIR OWN WORDS

'I'm Jonne Lövgren, a 61-year-old self-employed graphic designer from Fornby, Dalarna. I used to have a small apartment with no view in downtown Stockholm. I was always in the studio, or hurrying to clients or having lunches I didn't want. In winter I never saw the sun. We produced everything on paper in those days, with lettering sheets and marker pens. Then computers appeared and you could do everything with a mouse. I haven't used a marker pen for twenty years. And then someone wonderful invented e-mail and suddenly I didn't even need to be in the city. I moved back "home" to my little village in Dalarna. Here, I can finish a job for a client, send it down the phone lines, and be swimming in the lake three minutes later!'

This was a difficult time for Sweden. However, Swedes have always embraced new technologies, and as old industries, like ship-building, disappeared, new opportunities arose. Many young people especially have started their own businesses in the new computer-based media, entertainment and service industries. And now Swedes living in the far north are no longer at such a disadvantage. Online home-based working means you do not have to live in Stockholm to have an exciting, well-paid job.

▶ *The microchip-based working environment of the future. Swedish companies usually favour open-plan offices.*

# 9

# The Way Ahead

In the mid-nineteenth century most Swedes lived as part of large families. They inhabited small, isolated villages and worked the land and forests with simple tools in all weather conditions. They were a poor, hard-working, religious people with limited ambitions. Few foreigners lived here and the country was remote and inward-looking.

At the start of the twenty-first century Sweden is very different. Few people now work the land, and those who do use sophisticated equipment and make a good living. Families are small and everyone is better off and healthier. Sweden today is no longer so inward-looking. It is a fully participating member of the European Union and has a huge immigrant population. There is a flourishing tourist industry.

Swedes enjoy a very high standard of living. Industry is modern and efficient, and the economy is strong. All young people learn foreign languages and most like to travel outside Sweden. Practically everyone speaks English. Modern Sweden is a multi-racial country and is rapidly becoming a multi-cultural one.

▼ *Peace sculpture situated outside Malmö's central railway station.*

## IN THEIR OWN WORDS

'I'm Lisa Carlberg from Skellefteå. I'm 23 and work as a post girl. Well, I'm pretty certain about one thing: I won't still be delivering letters in ten years time. I hated school. I never did any work and left as soon as I could – with no qualifications. But the great thing about Sweden is that you can go back to school whenever you like and finish your studies. I'm starting school again – seven years late – in August. I'm ready for it now. I'm gonna be a local politician, maybe even an MP. There are important issues up here in the north – unemployment, population decline, things like that – they've forgotten about down in Stockholm. It's always Europe this and Europe that. And money for immigrants and bridges to Denmark. We have to remember that we're Swedish, too.'

So, is Sweden today as Swedish as it was a century ago? The challenge for Swedes is to maintain their identity when so much change is influenced by other countries and cultures. The Swedish language will have to survive alongside English. Swedes may become officially bi-lingual in your lifetime.

And how will Sweden's traditions of modesty and industriousness, of fairness and tolerance be influenced by the new Swedes, half of whom are now born to non-Swedish parents? The new region of Malmö and Copenhagen shows one way in which political and economic co-operation can bring important benefits to both parties without destroying the identity of either.

▶ *The Swedish flag still flies over every city. But it has been joined by those of EU partner states that have an increasing influence over life in Sweden today.*

# Glossary

**Allemansrätten** The Right of Common Access is a Swedish law which gives everyone the right to walk anywhere in the countryside, even across private land, and to take, for example, berries and mushrooms freely from the forest.

**Archipelago** A group of small islands, such as those along the Swedish west coast, in the North Sea, or those to the east of Stockholm, in the Baltic Sea.

**Arctic Circle** The area of the world around the North Pole.

**Asylum seekers** Foreign nationals who are persecuted for their political and/or religious beliefs in their own country and who, therefore, seek asylum (protection) in another country.

**Baltic States** Estonia, Latvia and Lithuania, countries which lie on the east shore of the Baltic Sea.

**Barnombudsmannen** The Children's Ombudsman.

**Depression** A period of no economic growth, which can result in increased unemployment.

**Guest workers** Foreigners with particular work skills who are encouraged to become temporary immigrants to fill gaps in the labour market.

**Gulf Stream** A warm ocean current which flows north-eastwards from the Gulf of Mexico towards northern Europe. The Gulf Stream affects the climates of the British Isles and western Scandinavia particularly, making them warmer than they would otherwise be.

**Hydroelectric** Electrical power made by harnessing the energy of running water.

**Lagom** The Swedish word for 'just about right', which represents an important social value in Swedish society.

**Lucia** Sweden's festival of light celebrated on 13 December. Lucia, the Queen of Light, visits Swedes to bring a little light in the middle of their long, dark winter. Lucia is celebrated in homes, schools and at workplaces. A young girl is chosen to be Lucia. She dresses in a long white dress with a red sash and wears a crown of candles. The celebrations are complete when Lucia and her helpers sing traditional songs and serve coffee and spiced biscuits to everyone present.

**Lutheran** A Protestant branch of the Christian religion.

**Multi-national** Companies which operate globally and are not limited to doing business in their country of origin.

**Nationalization** The policy of the government taking over the ownership and running of key industries.

**NATO** The North Atlantic Treaty Organization was set up in 1949 by a group of European countries (excluding Sweden and all the members of the Soviet bloc of eastern European countries) together with Canada and the USA. Each agreed to help other NATO members if they were attacked by an aggressor.

**Neutral** Not officially supporting either side in a war or other dispute, and, therefore, not actively participating (i.e. fighting) in such a war.

**Ombudsman** An independent, government-appointed arbitrator or judge.

**Right wing** A term used for conservative politicians.

**Sami** Native people of Lapland.

**Social benefit** Money paid by the state to help those who are unemployed, disabled or too ill to work.

**Social Democratic Party** Sweden's equivalent of the Labour Party in the United Kingdom.

**Taiga** A transitional area of plant growth characterized by scattered trees lying between the Arctic tundra and boreal coniferous forests.

**Terawatt (TW)** Unit of electricity production. It equals $10^{12}$ watts, or a thousand billion watts.

**Viking** Scandinavian warriors who sailed to nearby countries to invade and colonize them, between AD 800–1060 .

# Further Information

## Books to read

*Maypoles, Crayfish and Lucia – Swedish Holidays and Traditions* by Jan-Öjvind Swahn (trans. Roger Tanner) (The Swedish Institute, 1994)

*Nations of the World: Sweden* by Robbie Butler (Raintree, 2004)

*Spotlight on Sweden* by Hans-Ingvar Johnsson (The Swedish Institute, 1999)

*Sweden, children's folder* (English language edition) by Lars Forsberg (The Swedish Institute, 2001)

*Sweden in Figures* Annual summary of statistical data from the Statistical Yearbook of Sweden (Statistics Sweden [Central Bureau of Statistics] Örebro, Sweden, annually)

## Note about the Swedish alphabet and pronunciation of Swedish words

The Swedish alphabet contains 28 letters. Modern Swedish does not normally use 'w' (except in surnames, such as Wiklund, and in foreign words, such as Volkswagen), but there are three letters not found in English. They are å, ä and ö. These are letters in their own right, with their own pronunciations and place in the alphabet, after 'z'. They cannot be replaced by 'a' and 'o'. They are usually described in English as 'a' with a small circle over it, 'a' with two dots and 'o' with two dots. They are pronounced, approximately, as follows:

å     like eau in the French word beaux (example, Luleå)

ä     like air in the word pair (example, Täby)

ö     like ur in the word purr (example, Malmö)

Thus, the roughly correct pronunciation of the following words is

    fält (meaning a field or meadow) felt

    smörgås (meaning an open sandwich) smurrgoas

Remember, if you want to look up år ('year') in a Swedish dictionary, you will find it after 'z'. Älv ('river') will be found under the next letter – ä. Likewise, if you use a Swedish telephone directory to look up Sven Åkermark's phone number, it will be after 'z' and before 'ä'.

## Places to visit

**IKEA furniture stores** (typical Swedish cafeteria food; visit at Christmas for traditional Swedish decorations and food types and brands not otherwise imported).

**Jorvik Viking Centre, York.**

**Sweden House**, Kungsträdgården, Stockholm. The central location of this purpose-built information centre for visitors to Stockholm makes it an absolutely invaluable location for information, tickets, merchandise and souvenirs. The second floor Sweden Bookshop offers a fine range of titles on all aspects of Swedish life, history and culture in all principal world languages.

## Useful addresses

The Embassy of Sweden
11 Montagu Place
London W1H 2AL
The embassy can provide information about Swedish National Day (6 June) when there are occasional celebrations in London.

Radio Sweden International
Broadcasts about Sweden, worldwide, daily, in English

Swedish Travel and Tourism Council
5 Upper Montagu Street
London W1H 2AG
Information and brochure line 00 800 3080 3080 (freephone)
Tel: 020 7870 5600
e-mail: info@swetourism.org.uk

The Swedish Information Service
One Dag Hammarskjold Plaza
New York
NY 10017-2201
USA

# Index

Page numbers in **bold** refer to photographs, maps or statistics panels.